Frame and Mount the Sky

poems by

**Donelle Dreese, Karen George,
Nancy Jentsch & Taunja Thomson**

Finishing Line Press
Georgetown, Kentucky

Frame and Mount the Sky

Copyright © 2017 by Donelle Dreese, Karen George, Nancy Jentsch, Taunja Thomson
ISBN 978-1-63534-232-1 First Edition
All rights reserved under International and Pan-American Copyright Conventions.
No part of this book may be reproduced in any manner whatsoever without written permission from the publisher, except in the case of brief quotations embodied in critical articles and reviews.

ACKNOWLEDGMENTS

Many thanks to the publications in which original versions of the following poems appeared:

Accents Publishing blog, "Monet's Haystacks, the End of the Summer at Giverny, 1891"
Aeqai's Art for a Better World, "Monet's Ice Floes on the Seine at Bougival, 1867"
Canary, "End of the Road"
Ekphrastic Review, "Monet's The Magpie, 1872"
Fourth River, "Framed and Mounted"
New Verse News, "Politicians Discussing Global Warming"
Tupelo Press 30-30 website, "Monet's Rouen Cathedral, Bright Sun, Harmony in Blue and Gold, 1892-1894," and "Monet's Rough Sea at Etretat, 1868"

Publisher: Leah Maines
Editor: Christen Kincaid
Cover Art: Karen George
Author Photos:
    Donelle Dreese's photo: Jason Sheldon
    Karen George's photo: Karen George
    Nancy Jentsch's photo: Tim Sofranko
    Taunja Thomson's photo: Ben Von Handorf
Cover Design: Elizabeth Maines McCleavy

Printed in the USA on acid-free paper.
Order online: www.finishinglinepress.com
    also available on amazon.com

Author inquiries and mail orders:
Finishing Line Press
P. O. Box 1626
Georgetown, Kentucky 40324
U. S. A.

Table of Contents

Monet's Meditation, Madame Monet on the Sofa, 1871 1
Monet's Rough Sea at Etretat, 1868 2
Monet's Storm off the Coast of Belle-Ile, 1886 3
Monet's Ice Floes on the Seine at Bougival, 1867 4
Monet's The Magpie, 1872 5
A haiku about Monet's Haystacks, the End of the
    Summer at Giverny, 1891 6
Monet's Rouen Cathedral: Bright Sun, Harmony in
    Blue and Gold, 1892-1894 7
Musing upon "Ladies in Blue" (a Minoan Fresco) 8
Sea Witch (Frank Frazetta, 1966) 9
Colorado Moon Barrette (a Gift from Sheila) 10
Guardians of the Gateway (William Ricketts
    Sanctuary (Melbourne, Australia) 11
Gulnare of the Sea (Maxfield Parrish, 1909) 12
Sun Goddess (Frank Frazetta, circa 1973) 13
Great Blue Heron (Caia Koopman) 14
End of the Road (Isaac Cordal, Cement Eclipses) 15
The Green Grave (Isaac Cordal, Cement Eclipses) 16
Waiting for Climate Change (Isaac Cordal, Cement
    Eclipses) 17
The Mechanics of Kissing (Isaac Cordal, Cement
    Eclipses) 18
Politicians Discussing Global Warming (Isaac Cordal,
    Cement Eclipses) 19
Remembering Fruit (Isaac Cordal, Cement Eclipses) 20
Framed and Mounted (Isaac Cordal, Cement Eclipses) 21
The Blue Rider (Wassily Kandinsky, 1903) 22
Kahnpartie (Gabriele Münter, 1910) 23
Horse Unharnessed (Blaues Pferd I, Franz Marc, 1911) 24
Red Deer II (Franz Marc, 1912) 25
Mein Garten (Gabriele Münter, 1931) 26
Window Framed (Breakfast of the Birds,
    Gabriele Münter, 1934) 27
A Matter of Art (Jawlensky und Werefkin,
    Gabriele Münter, 1909) 28

Monet's Meditation, Madame Monet on the Sofa, 1871

Sun through muslin sheers
falls on Camille's face.
Velvet dress   black   heavy
mottled midnight-blue
might be the effect of light—
Monet's mania.

Behind her, corner of a marble fireplace
mantel holds a mirror, vase, bellows,
on the wall the bottom edge of a gilt frame,
hint of blue the painting contains.

Did she tire of posing?
Hair pinned at her crown, head bowed
half in shadow, glazed
numb from money worries,
somber as if she glimpsed her future.

Seated on floral chintz, green, cream
red that matches the rug and bow
knotted at her neck, the book
cupped loosely in her lap
like an uncooked egg.

Seven years later, she gives birth to a second son, and dies eighteen
months later, only 32

Karen George

Monet's Rough Sea at Etretat, 1868

Your language
medley of smashed sounds
liquid loneliness ramming the rocks

What drew us
to the desolation
of your pelagic world

You thunder through twilight
scour the continental shelf
belly to belly in the rub of time

A found poem from "The Wellfleet Whale" by Stanley Kunitz

Karen George

Monet's Storm off the Coast of Belle-Ile, 1886

Nothing but sea, sky, boulders.
Very little light
no boat to heave into
no shore for collapse
sky darker steel-blue than the sea
wind-struck waves painted
with long strokes drag you
toward boulders that jut
smaller ones mounded
shredding blue into white
like rows of teeth.

A shudder passes through me as I recall
rafting rapid after rapid
whitewater pitching us past crag faces—
blades our guide warned of getting wedged
against, trapped underwater
if slung overboard.

In the painting center a channel
appears safer though dark shadows
hint sharp edges you don't see
beneath slashing waves—
all dizzying motion
but the rooted stones.

Karen George

Monet's Ice Floes on the Seine at Bougival, 1867

Steel gray sky and wide river consume
half the painting. Not much more than smudges,
the stooped figures look like spent matchsticks
leaning this way and that.

They've come to the jagged edge for water.
Two wait their turn behind a woman
who kneels with a pail submerged,
the white of her bonnet dissolved
against the snow-choked ground.

She dips her pail in the river,
gazes past ice slabs to the opposite shore,
its dark-snarled poplars mirrored
in the river like nubs of rotted teeth
or haunts who gathered water there year after year.

The pale sun provides no warmth,
her cloak not thick enough.
Hired out at fourteen, twice daily she plods
to the Seine, tries not to think about the soiled path
behind her, how far she must go, handles dug into her palms.

How easy to lean
toward the flow, slip
into the liquid bed.
Cold creeps up her arm, hand held
by the frigid river forever.

Karen George

Monet's The Magpie, 1872

A house behind trees
steep-pitched roof, red chimneys
fence and gate horizontal
at the scene's center—
caesura from white, silver, gold
snow which cushions, catches
in crooks. Swirled strokes convey
layers, echo arched tree limbs.

On the top rung of a warped gate
a magpie basks, beak cocked in silhouette,
tail feathers angled right,
same as shadows that point
to the canvas bottom corner
where Monet's signature slants.

Past the magpie's umbra, dark tracks
boot or hoof, walk off
the painting, invite you to enter
feet tingling.

Distant fields stretch, fuse
with sky, late day sun unseen
reflects from every surface
onto your face
imprinting.

Karen George

A haiku about Monet's Haystacks

a vision ringing
golden blue fiery yellow
shadow light nearer

A haiku about Monet's *Haystacks, the End of the Summer at Giverny*, 1891, found in Tomas Transtromer's "After the Attack," translated by Robert Bly

Karen George

**Monet's Rouen Cathedral: Bright Sun, Harmony in Blue
and Gold, 1892-1894**

Blue softest with gold
striped silken from liquid light
that falls to its palace and gothic parapets
sacred elevation of nectar
the burning heart of honey
palpitates the statues
infinite tongues
a hive of honeycombs

A found poem from Pablo Neruda's "Ode to the Bee," translated by
Stephen Mitchell

Karen George

Musing upon "Ladies in Blue"
(a Minoan Fresco)

Three women gossip against
field of blue
sky:

three women with ebony hair
                        pearly coiffes
                tiered bracelets   amber sleeves
                      time on their white hands
                              which flutter.

I picture them holding lace handkerchiefs
                (damsels?)
or cigarettes (vamps?).

       Time has erased them
       from the waist down
                yet their eyes are still bright
                their smiles
                        solid.

                                          Taunja Thomson

Sea Witch
    (Frank Frazetta, 1966)

Two silver snakes fly
from her outstretched arms.
She: white as moon
bathed in gauzy pall
hair Nix-black
a thick dark wave
roiling in wind
gold on her ears
wrists neck slung
from her waist.
She commands
mottled clouds
fierce ocean
of azure and lapis
now stained with the patina
of storm.
Below the rock
on which she stands
something dark
dappled tentacled
rises winds itself
around her craggy dais;
behind her a leviathan
lizard hoists itself
pulling veins of ocean
in its wake.
She basks in dominion.

                                          Taunja Thomson

Colorado Moon Barrette
(a Gift from Sheila)

Rough oval: inside
quarter moon with sharp
nose, thin smile, arched eyebrow—
mischief is afoot
just like I like it.
A wave rises, splits in two,
heads for moon, touches it
briefly.
Oak-colored lines, irregular,
sparse, pierce darker, lightweight wood
making it look old, a thing
passed down.
She knows I dream
of my grandmother
often.
Final touch: smooth, tapering
stick rolling through the whole of it
keeping all in place
despite its churning, chaotic
nature.
Good to have a friend
who knows you well.

Taunja Thomson

Guardians of the Gateway
    (William Ricketts Sanctuary, Melbourne, Australia)

White path narrows:
gentlemen   gods
of the old world
their Neptunian beards curling
windblown in rock
arms muscled   chests bronzed
with age
rise out of mossy
boulders
on either side
their backs laurel green.
Beyond them:
ferns   lichen-skirted trees
patches of sky
through emerald-encrusted
branches. Yet
you pause
between these guardians
enamored
before stepping
into paradise proper.

                                          Taunja Thomson

Gulnare of the Sea
    (Maxfield Parrish, 1909)

Wrapped in gold and lavender
she leans over sundry amphora:
rough   the color of sunset sand
shiny   marred with patches of age
and the small container
that fits her white hand.
Her fawn-brown hair spilling
over her back, she leans down
encouraging the smoke
that rises from a vessel
perhaps preparing to harvest
its contents.
To what purpose?
Only the amaranthine flowers
surrounding her head
like a halo
know.

                                            Taunja Thomson

Sun Goddess
    (Frank Frazetta, circa 1973)

Light dances around her
radiates from her
to sun
and back
upon her outstretched arms
upturned face.
Blade in hand
saber tooth by her side
they stand on jutting rock.
With necklace of bone
she drips
gold
from her thighs.
Orb sheds light
on her modest breasts
wide hips
on the back of the beast
turning him red.
Black hair flies out behind her
strong brushstrokes
swept up in the joy
of solitude and self-determination.

                                        Taunja Thomson

Great Blue Heron
    (Caia Koopman)

Girl with body of wraith
slick hair   bangs swept
over forehead
(ebony on alabaster)
stands against the palest
of green skies
flecked with stars.
Gray of storm seeps in
as flowers fall
from her hair.
On her chest
a heart aflame:
white wings
a keyhole.

Over her shoulder
leans a heron
his blue feathers echoing
her tears
his neck snaking
up her thin arms
his beak piercing
her neck.

From below
a tentative
verdurous
vine
touches her.

Taunja Thomson

End of the Road
    (Isaac Cordal, Cement Eclipses)

From the wide berth of the road
you can see his miniature life

hands folded behind his back to consider
the rock and monolith of it all

a sculpted tiny man swallowed
by stark gravel and stone.

At the end of the road
there is no Emerald City

only a wizard-less nuclear power plant
smoking a twin death brew

big as a country
gray as dead elephants.

But the sky sweeps a bunting blue
and soul-deep green trees border the road

as if to say

the sublime streets where we all live
lead to the same blank, immaculate accident.

                                        Donelle Dreese

The Green Grave
(Isaac Cordal, Cement Eclipses)

In a stone city, you stand sobbing
bearing a bruised briefcase, a suit
the color of an overcast sky.

The only hair left on your head
creates a skirt along your occipital ridge,
a gray curtain for a short neck.

Floating in this rubble sea is a green grave,
the last patch of grass to survive the laying,
but it too waits for the mortar to pour.

The white cross has been staked
into its tender loam and rests,
mysterious as an unknown soldier.

Little man, you peer into the scrap
of grass to pay homage maybe,
to remember your boyhood knee stains.

Perhaps you recall Walt Whitman
from a college class you never wanted to take.

You want to learn something about softness
in the eleventh hour of your concrete life.

Donelle Dreese

Waiting for Climate Change
    (Isaac Cordal, Cement Eclipses)

Here's a rumpled beach
dune frays at the back rising
hotels looming on the horizon.

Ten tall wooden pedestals
serve as poles made into lookouts
puncturing a sunny sky, a resort sky.

On top of each pedestal
little gray men are waiting
for the water to siege.

The ocean keeps its distance
white-capped and hushing
no fear for miles.

But the men have their cell phones
survival gear wrapping
their waists as they electrify time.

When the surge makes landfall
the phones will hum
the pedestals will save them.

Pedestals that will snap into twigs.
Phones that will fizzle in Arctic foam.

                                          Donelle Dreese

The Mechanics of Kissing
(Isaac Cordal, Cement Eclipses)

Love blooms in a contaminated city.

Infections, poised side by side,
the lovers wear gas masks
as if they just uttered "I do,"
but no one hears them. No one
knows who they are.

The ashen wedding dress is draped in soot
and the rose bouquet barely beams red
during its polluted attempt to stun.

When it is time to kiss,
they have a choice, nuzzle
the noses of the grimy masks,
(two machines bumping in a factory),
or risk it all for a tender, pink mouth.

Donelle Dreese

Politicians Discussing Global Warming
(Isaac Cordal, Cement Eclipses)

The billions beneath have drowned
leaving tiny pink congressional skulls
to emerge as pimples in a water-fat city.

They will not survive. They are swamped
in thawed Arctic Sea ice uttering bloated
bubbles that debate and float away.

They ascend on stacks of money and hover
the Atlantic waves, awaiting the final swoon
praying for a proposal to surface.

The discussion gurgles on and on
through puffed, water-inflated robes.
The last life-preserver goes to the whitest scalp.

Donelle Dreese

Remembering Fruit
(Isaac Cordal, Cement Eclipses)

The world is a bald wonder
debarked smooth wood flesh
barely a bump where a limb
used to plank toward green,
but at least we can stand tall
balanced on a walnut stump
looking down at the concrete
remembering fruit.

Donelle Dreese

Framed and Mounted
    (Isaac Cordal, Cement Eclipses)

A lone painting of a landscape
decks an urban brick wall.

It has leaning trees and a countryside
flickering through blue haze.

Two street-side immobilized men ponder
as if touring a back-alley Smithsonian.

One holds his chin, remembers hillsides
contemplates the anatomy of leaves.

The other clutches a briefcase
moans for grass and birdsong.

Someday we will frame and mount the sky
feel its canvas, smell its paint, bank our dreams

on wooden squares from art supply stores
pretend we hear bees circling the hive.

                                    Donelle Dreese

The Blue Rider
(Wassily Kandinsky, 1903)

The century's new
but poems still rhyme
melodies find their way home
and Kandinsky's horseman starts his race.

Blue-robed and riding art's *limes*
he canters across sunbeams
straddling a cloud-cream stallion.

We see him only for an instant
caught left of center in midstride
against a freshly mown field.

Quick daubs of blue and white,
he is dubbed *The Blue Rider*,
and races fast, focused on the century's unfolding,
collecting companions who take his name.

From his saddle they paint essence, no longer reality
and gallop from shadowless landscapes
past floating churches to yellow cows.

Until finally, the herald's flight fulfilled
he dismounts, disavows rhyme and melody, even essence
onto a canvas with no name.

Limes means border and often refers to Roman frontier fortifications.

Kandinsky's work *Untitled Watercolor,* 1910 is considered by many to be the first work of abstract art.

Nancy Jentsch

Kahnpartie
    (Gabriele Münter, 1910)

Carrying only canvas and oils in tubes
(last century's legacy to landscape artists)
Münter makes a boat on the Staffelsee her studio
where she can be brushed by the lake's breeze
        sense fish and fir
        hear water paddled
        discover the blueness of the Alps
        echo it in Kandinsky's eyes
                as if our gaze bores through him
                for another glimpse
                of the mountains at his back

                                    Nancy Jentsch

Horse Unharnessed
    (Blaues Pferd I, Franz Marc, 1911)

The horse stands bold yet brooding,
distinguished against

a background of choreographed colors,
cool and warm in turn,

which radiate in mountains
and mist as if a Romantic painting.

Exotic plants curve,
wedding foreground

with ambience of art-nouveau.
But the horse maintains his modernity,

hooves hovering.
Careful to cast no shadow

he nods a noble assent
to the approaching age of abstract art.

Did I mention the horse was blue?

                                      Nancy Jentsch

Red Deer II
    (Franz Marc, 1912)

Form two deer and brush bodies with red-orange.
Soften with white fur.

Position heads in opposing directions.
Let them sniff what deer sniff.

Break one deer's plane to show head in profile
while body captures a graceful bend.

Follow front deer's gaze to upper right.
Plot parallel path to lead viewer's eye.

Round mountains and paint point-tipped leaves
to echo body curves and acute angle ears.

Bring red-orange to flashpoint
with complements of rain-washed green and bold blue.

Contemplate a composition as careful in its creation
as nature is resplendent in its randomness.

                                            Nancy Jentsch

Mein Garten
    (Gabriele Münter, 1931)

Red-dressed and neatly shuttered in green
above a tall rogue sunflower,
you look down on ordered garden rows,
paint them in bold strokes and tones.

Green crests in primary colors
echoing right to left like pealing bells.
Stone-lined path watched by that lone sunflower
invites a stroll toward the sun.

Johannes nods. His late summer harvest
seeks shade under high-grown border grasses.
Two more sunflowers end the path,
obeisant to the western sky.

The horizon, devoid of detail, releases you
to attend to the *Augenweide* your garden offers,
where eyes can graze on planned rows
sprinkled with splashes of chance.

Years later, your delight,
reflected on canvas and named *Mein Garten*,
extends from your window-framed gaze
to the gratitude of mine.

An *Augenweide* is a pleasurable view, literally a pasture for the eyes.

Nancy Jentsch

Window Framed
    (Breakfast of the Birds, Gabriele Münter, 1934)

I can learn about birds from books
but to hear them chirp or chatter or chuckle
is to sense their essence
their interlocking
with moment and place.

And if you want to know me
would the writer's bio
solve the puzzle
or could you extract more essentials
by pondering my poetry?

So what better self-portrait
than one that frames the artist seated with back to us
looking out a window at birds on snow-frosted limbs
or a journeyman seen from the rear scanning
mist-filled valleys under a storm-laden sky?

                                            Nancy Jentsch

A Matter of Art
(Jawlensky und Werefkin, Gabriele Münter, 1909)

Invited by the hillside to a windy afternoon with friends,
the artist at her easel paints in calming colors,
edged Gaugin-like in black.
A glint of *Alpenglühen* crosses the canvas,
overflowing into hat and flower,
gold and pink disarming
the dominance of grass and mountain.

Drawn into cool colors by warm but featureless faces
against a classic background of land and sky
we wonder what the reclining couple whispered,
whether their eyes were closed,
if they had picked pink flowers from the meadow
to adorn Marianne's turn-of-the-century hat.

The answers don't matter.
The questions do.

Alpenglühen is a meteorological phenomenon that translates as Alpine glow.

Nancy Jentsch

Notes

Sincerest gratitude to sculptor Isaac Cordal for his *Cement Eclipses: Small Interventions in the Big City*. Cordal's little grey men have appeared in cities around the world as part of an urban art series.
~ **Donelle Dreese**

I first heard the term "ekphrastic" while completing my MFA in Writing at Spalding University, and wrote my first poem about a work of art as an assignment. In 2012, when I traveled to Paris with Spalding's Summer Residency Program, my love for Impressionist Art was rekindled by a visit to the Musee d' Orsay, where I viewed the Monet paintings written about in this chapbook.
~ **Karen George**

The seven final poems in this book were inspired by the paintings of a group of German and Russian artists called Der Blaue Reiter (The Blue Rider). The artists worked in and around Munich, Germany in the years leading up to the First World War.
~ **Nancy Jentsch**

I would like to thank artists Frank Frazetta, Maxfield Parrish, Caia Koopman, and the creators of the Guardians of the Gateway sculpture, as well as the ever-fascinating Minoan civilization and my friend Sheila Ruark for providing the inspiration for the poems I've written for *Frame and Mount the Sky*.
~ **Taunja Thomson**

Donelle Dreese is a Professor of English at Northern Kentucky University. She is the author of three collections of poetry, *Sophrosyne* (Aldrich Press), *A Wild Turn* (Finishing Line) and *Looking for A Sunday Afternoon* (Pudding House). Donelle is also the author of the YA novella *Dragonflies in the Cowburbs* (Anaphora Literary) and the ecofiction novels *Deep River Burning* (WiDo Publishing) and *Cave Walker* (Moon Willow Press). Her poetry and fiction have appeared in a wide variety of literary journals including *Blue Lyra Review, Roanoke Review, Louisville Review,* and *Quiddity International.*
Website: http://www.donelledreese.com

Karen George, author of *Into the Heartland* (Finishing Line Press, 2011), *Inner Passage* (Red Bird Chapbooks, 2014), *Swim Your Way Back* (Dos Madres Press, 2014), *The Seed of Me* (Finishing Line Press, 2015), and *The Fire Circle* (Blue Lyra Press, 2016). She has received grants from Kentucky Foundation for Women and Kentucky Arts Council. Her work has appeared in *Naugatuck River Review, Adirondack Review, America, Louisville Review, Blue Lyra Review,* and *Still*. She holds an MFA in Writing from Spalding University, reviews poetry at http://readwritepoetry.blogspot.com/, and is co-founder and fiction editor of the online journal, *Waypoints*: http://www.waypointsmag.com/.
Her website is: http://karenlgeorge.snack.ws/.

Nancy Jentsch lives in northern Kentucky where she has taught German and Spanish for over thirty years. Since 1985 she has published scholarly articles, short stories and poems in journals such as the *Aurorean, Journal of Kentucky Studies, Panoply* and *Eclectica*. Her chapbook *Authorized Visitors* is forthcoming with Cherry Grove Collections, an imprint of WordTech Communications. Recently she has been inspired by the boldly innovative art of the group of artists known as The Blue Rider and has visited museums in Germany and the United States to better acquaint herself with their artwork.

Taunja Thomson's poetry has appeared in *Wild Age Press, Panoply Magazine, Potomac, Crawl Space,* and *The Ekphrastic Review*. Two of her poems have been nominated for Pushcart Awards: "Seahorse and Moon" in 2005 and "I Walked Out in January" in 2016. She has a writer's page at https://www.facebook.com/TaunjaThomsonWriter. A worshiper of nature, her summers are filled with water gardening, and her winters are spent obsessively feeding the birds and other wildlife that appear in her one-acre slice of heaven, a field.

www.ingramcontent.com/pod-product-compliance
Lightning Source LLC
LaVergne TN
LVHW041511070426
835507LV00012B/1498